HEALTH AND FITNESS

Style Secrets for Girls

STEPHANIE TURNBULL

A+

Smart Apple Media

Published by Smart Apple Media, an imprint of Black Rabbit Books
P.O. Box 3263, Mankato, Minnesota 56002
www.blackrabbitbooks.com

Library of Congress Cataloging-in-Publication Data

Turnbull, Stephanie.
Health and fitness : style secrets for girls / Stephanie Turnbull.
pages cm.—(Girl talk)
Includes index.
Summary: "A fun magazine-like book for preteen and teen girls on ways to be healthy. Includes information on hygiene, eating right, fitness, and well-being"—Provided by publisher.
ISBN 978-1-59920-947-0 (library binding)
1. Girls—Life skills guides—Juvenile literature. 2. Girls—Health and hygiene—Juvenile literature. I. Title.
HQ777.T87 2014
613'.04242--dc23
                              2012050411

Created by Appleseed Editions Ltd,
Designed and illustrated by Guy Callaby
Edited by Mary-Jane Wilkins

Picture credits
t = top, b = bottom, l = left, r = right, c = center
title page R. Gino Santa Maria/Shutterstock; page 2t TongChuwit/Shutterstock, b iStockphoto/Thinkstock; 3 Lasse Kristensen/Shutterstock; 4l cabania, r eurobanks/both Shutterstock; 5l Denis Babenko, r Andre Blais/both Shutterstock, b Hemera/Thinkstock; 6t Ilya Andriyanov, c alexkatkov/both Shutterstock; 7t Rafa Irusta, l gosphotodesign, cr Luis Santos, b Cameramannz/all Shutterstock; 8t Mihai Simonia, b Svetlana Lukienko/both Shutterstock; 9 Tomislav Pinter/Shutterstock; 10t gosphotodesign, l Yeko Photo Studio, b Juriah Mosin/all Shutterstock; 11t CREATISTA, r Tami Freed/both Shutterstock; 12t HLPhoto/Shutterstock; 14l CGissemann, r AISPIX by Image Source/both Shutterstock; 15 stockcreations/Shutterstock; 16t Lana K, bl & r Nitr/all Shutterstock; 17 drfelice/Shutterstock; 18 Monkey Business Images/Shutterstock; 19 iStockphoto/Thinkstock; 20 Petunyia/Shutterstock; 21b Jacek Chabraszewski, r Chris Turner/both Shutterstock; 22 AISPIX by Image Source/Shutterstock; 23t Yuri Arcurs, b Anatoliy Samara/both Shutterstock; 24t Polka Dot Images/Thinkstock, c Jaimie Duplass/Shutterstock; 26t YanLev, b samotrebizan/both Shutterstock; 27t Chamille White, b Vlue/both Shutterstock; 28t mast3r/Shutterstock, bl Jupiterimages/Thinkstock, r Vibrant Image Studio/Shutterstock; 29t Szasz-Fabian Ilka Erika, r Netfalls - Remy Musser, b Garsya/all Shutterstock; 30t Joerg Beuge, b Raymond Kasprzak/both Shutterstock; 31 iStockphoto/Thinkstock; 32 Jaren Jai Wicklund/Shutterstock

Front cover: iStockphoto/Thinkstock

Printed in the United States at Corporate Graphics in North Mankato, Minnesota.
PO DAD5005a
102013

9 8 7 6 5 4 3 2

Contents

Smart Living

Being fit and healthy makes you feel good and look great. It involves looking after your body, eating well, and getting active. This book is packed with tips and tricks to improve your health and fitness—and help you have fun at the same time!

Enjoy Yourself

Health and fitness always go together. Leading a healthy lifestyle gives you lots of energy to exercise, while plenty of exercise keeps your body growing well and working fantastically. The key is to choose healthy foods and activities that you enjoy, so you feel like you're treating your body, not punishing it!

Body Benefits

Regular exercise strengthens your heart, lungs, muscles, and bones. It boosts your **immune system** to fight illness and prevent disease, and stops your body from storing excess fat. Exercise can improve **digestion** and **circulation**. It even helps you sleep better.

The more energy you use, the more you have! You'll also be alert and able to concentrate well.

Body Facts

Being fit lets you bend and stretch your body more. Some people can hook their feet behind their ears!

Many of your bones won't stop growing until you're about 20.

When you exercise, your body produces chemicals called endorphins that make you feel happy.

Pssst... Hot Tip!

Look out for these tips throughout the book. They give you all kinds of extra ideas and advice for keeping fit and healthy.

Freshening Up

One of the simplest but most important ways to stay healthy is to keep clean. Regular washing and basic body maintenance gets rid of dirt and harmful germs that cause colds, flu, tummy bugs, and other illnesses.

Hand Hygiene

The most common way that germs spread is by hand—so always wash yours before preparing or eating food, after touching animals, handling anything dirty, or blowing your nose, and of course, after going to the bathroom. Always use soap!

A daily bath or shower is great, but hair doesn't need washing every day.

When washing, don't forget the backs of your hands...

...between your fingers...

...and your thumbs.

Splish Splash

Exercise makes you hot and sweaty, so always take a shower or bath afterward. Wash well after swimming, also, to get rid of pool chemicals. Dry off carefully so your skin doesn't become chapped and sore.

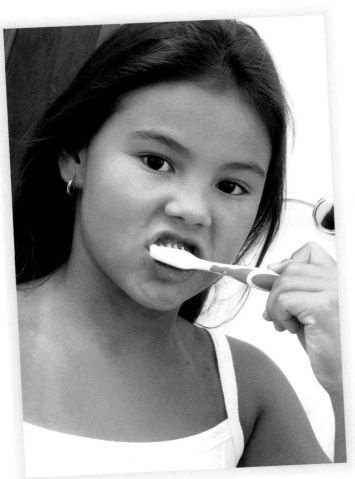

Use clean towels and washcloths to prevent spreading germs around.

Open Wide

Brushing your teeth twice a day keeps teeth and gums clean and healthy, and helps avoid bad breath, too. But don't attack your teeth with a violent burst of brushing. Take at least two minutes to gently massage the brush over every tooth surface.

Pssst... Keep your bedroom clean and tidy to cut down on germs, smells, and dust!

Yucky Stuff

Athlete's foot is an itchy, flaky skin disease that spreads in damp places, such as swimming pools.

A sneeze can send 40,000 tiny droplets of mucus spraying into the air.

Millions of germs grow under fingernails. Keep yours short, and clean them with a nail brush or cotton swab.

Pamper Time!

You've got beautifully clean skin, teeth, hair, and nails. Now how about having some fun so you feel (and smell) completely amazing?

Scented Soaks

If you have gift sets of bath bubbles, beads, soap, or salts, make time for a really long, luxurious bath and try them out. Alternatively, add a tablespoon of vanilla extract to your bath as you run the water to give it a delicate, delicious fragrance.

Pssst... Don't sprinkle loose herbs or flowers in your bath as you'll clog the drain. Make a bag for them from netting or a pair of tights.

Fresh or dried lavender gives baths a lovely scent.

Handmade Soap

To liven up plain, boring soaps, grate them into a large bowl.

This is a good way to use up tiny bars of soap.

Add a little water, a few drops at a time, until the mixture is soft enough to scrunch into a ball, like dough. Mix in a few drops of food coloring or perfume if you like. Mold the soap into shapes or press it into cookie cutters.

Don't use the grater, bowl, and cookie cutters for food preparation in the future.

Tea Treat

You can buy **conditioner** to give your hair extra strength and shine, but it's more fun to make your own! Green tea is a simple, non-messy natural conditioner. Put two green tea bags in a pitcher, carefully fill with boiling water, and leave for about 30 minutes to cool.

Remove the bags and pour the tea on clean, wet hair. Leave for about three minutes, then rinse off with cool water.

Don't Overdo It!

Although you want to smell fantastic, remember that using too many strongly scented lotions and perfumes can be overpowering—and they may irritate your skin. When trying new products, test them on a small patch of skin first to make sure you're not **allergic** to them.

Healthy Eating

Eating well is a vital part of being healthy. It helps your body grow properly and gives you strength and energy. Cuts, bruises, and broken bones heal faster, skin glows, and even your hair and nails look better.

Pick and Mix

The secret of healthy eating is to choose a variety of foods, so your body gets a good mix of **nutrients**. Foods such as bread, pasta, and rice are packed with energy-boosting **carbohydrates**, while meat, fish, eggs, and beans contain **protein**. You also need lots of **vitamins** and **minerals** from fruit, vegetables, and dairy products.

Use Your Head

There's no need to diet, and unless you have a food allergy, you don't have to obsess over food labels either—just think smart! Don't eat lots of fats or sugar, and choose fresh ingredients—the less **processed** your food is, the less salt, sugar, and fat it's likely to contain.

A baked potato with tuna and salad makes a healthy, filling lunch.

Pssst... Eat when you feel hungry, but stop as soon as you're full.

Snack Attack

Instead of snacking on candy bars or chips, try mixed seeds, dried fruit, or a smoothie (see page 16). They're more filling than you might think. Or why not make your own spiced popcorn? It contains no salt or sugar, unlike most pre-made popcorn.

1. Put ½ c. (100 g) popping corn into a big pan. Cover, and heat gently, shaking every so often.

Don't open the lid while the corn is popping!

2. After about five minutes the corn will start to pop. Keep heating and shaking the pan until the popping stops, then turn off the heat and leave for 30 seconds.

3. In another pan, gently heat a tablespoon of olive oil and a generous sprinkle of ground spices, such as curry powder, cinnamon, Chinese five-spice, or cayenne. Stir in handfuls of popcorn and toss to coat it in the mixture.

Experiment with a range of spices.

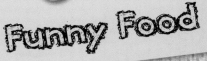

Insects such as ants, beetles, crickets, grubs, and scorpions are full of nutrients and can be eaten fried, roasted, or boiled!

Some types of carrots are purple.

Durians are southeast Asian fruits that stink of sweaty socks and rotten onions—but taste delicious!

Clever Cooking

Healthy meals shouldn't be boring! Find recipes at the library or online, and don't be afraid to try new or unusual foods. Remember to wash your hands first and ask for adult help, especially when using the oven.

Try couscous, a North African food made from wheat.

Roasted Veggie Wedges

If you find boiled vegetables bland, roast them instead—they taste delicious and are a great alternative to french fries.

1. Preheat the oven to 400°F (200°C). Chop vegetables into bite-sized chunks. Eggplant, zucchini, butternut squash, sweet potatoes (washed, but not peeled), carrots, and red onions all work well.

2. Put the vegetables in a roasting pan, drizzle on a tablespoon of olive oil, and turn to coat everything in oil. Cook for about 20 minutes.

Cherry tomatoes also roast well in only 10 minutes.

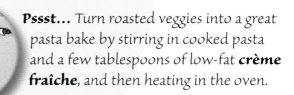

Pssst... Turn roasted veggies into a great pasta bake by stirring in cooked pasta and a few tablespoons of low-fat **crème fraîche**, and then heating in the oven.

Soy Salmon Bake

This tasty dish uses salmon, which is full of protein and **omega-3 fatty acids**, which are great for your heart. It serves four, but you can adapt it for more or fewer people.

You will need:
- ♥ 4 salmon fillets
- ♥ 1 red pepper, seeds removed
- ♥ 4 green onions, trimmed
- ♥ thumb-sized chunk of fresh ginger, peeled
- ♥ 1 carrot, peeled
- ♥ 2 Tbsp (30 mL) soy sauce
- ♥ juice of 1 orange
- ♥ 1 cup (250g) egg noodles
- ♥ 2 Tbsp (30 mL) sesame seeds

1. Preheat the oven to 400°F (200°C). Slice the vegetables thinly.

2. Tear four large pieces of tin foil and fold them in half. Place a salmon fillet in the middle of each and pile vegetable strips on top.

3. In a bowl, mix the soy sauce and orange juice. Roll up the edges of the foil, then pour some sauce over each fillet.

4. Scrunch the foil edges together over the fillets. Place in a baking pan and cook for 15 minutes.

5. Meanwhile, cook the egg noodles in boiling water according to the package instructions. Gently heat the sesame seeds in a frying pan until golden.

6. Drain the noodles and spoon into bowls. Lay the fillets on top, pour over any sauce from the foil, and sprinkle the sesame seeds on.

Fresh coriander makes a great finishing touch.

Sweet Stuff

There's no need to deny yourself dessert. Just eat small portions and choose light, low-fat, or reduced sugar options when you can. Even better, make your own desserts so you know exactly what is in them.

Fruity Yogurt

Fresh fruit tastes great on its own, but it's great to try something new. Heat berries or chopped fruit, such as mangoes, apples, or peaches, in a pan with a little water until soft. Purée the fruit in a blender and swirl into low-fat yogurt.

Try puréed fruit and yogurt with granola for a healthy breakfast.

Pssst... Don't forget that canned fruit is good for you, too—as long as there is no added sugar in the juice.

If you love ice cream, choose a small scoop in a cone rather than a big bowl.

Baked Bananas

Make a quick, tasty dessert by slicing a peeled banana lengthways. Lay it on aluminum foil with pecans, walnuts, or chopped dates, and drizzle a teaspoon of honey on top. Scrunch the foil into a packet, place on a baking pan, and cook at 400°F (200°C) for 15 minutes. Let cool before eating.

Chocolate Mousse

Try this for a special occasion! The secret ingredient is **tofu**, which creates a thick, creamy mixture without extra fat or sugar.

You will need:
- ♥ 7 oz. (200g) chocolate bar
- ♥ 12 oz. (340g) silken tofu
- ♥ 2 Tbsp (30 mL) sugar-free jam
- ♥ juice of ½ orange
- ♥ 1 tsp (5 mL) vanilla extract

1. Break the chocolate into chunks in a microwaveable bowl. Heat in 20-second bursts until melted, stirring regularly, so it doesn't burn. Be careful—the bowl will get hot.

2. Using a hand-held blender, purée the tofu until smooth and creamy. Add the jam, vanilla, and orange juice, then mix again.

Making individual portions stops you from eating too much.

3. Add the melted chocolate and purée until smooth and creamy. Pour into bowls or glasses, and refrigerate for at least two hours.

Drink Up!

Your body needs a constant supply of water to work properly, digest food, and grow. Without it, you become **dehydrated**, which makes you thirsty, weak, and dizzy. The best and easiest way to keep your water levels at their highest is by drinking plenty of it!

Get into the habit of bringing a small water bottle wherever you go.

Feeling Thirsty?

Fruit juices contain water, but make sure they don't also have added sugar. Instead of sodas, try herbal teas. They're much healthier, kinder to teeth, and can help freshen your breath, too.

Super Smoothies

Smoothies are really healthy drinks and are an easy way to consume lots of fruit in no time at all. They're also fun to make, as you can use whatever fruits you like. Blend chopped fruit on its own, or add milk and low-fat natural yogurt for a creamy milkshake.

Pssst... On hot days, why not try freezing fruit smoothies in popsicle molds?

Lemon Refresher

For a cool drink on a hot day, combine iced tea with homemade lemonade to make this sparkling brew. It's thirst-quenching and bursting with vitamin C.

1. *Pour boiling water over several fresh mint leaves, and let cool for about 10 minutes.*

2. *Squeeze the juice of a lemon into a glass, removing any seeds.*

3. *Strain the mint tea into the glass and stir in a teaspoon of sugar.*

4. *Chill in the fridge, then top off with carbonated water.*

Alternatively, leave out the sugar and top off with diet ginger ale.

Did You Know?

Energy drinks often contain caffeine, which can make you anxious, grumpy, and unable to sleep at night.

Every day your body loses more than 2 qt. (2L) of water, which needs replacing from food and drinks.

A can of cola contains about 8 tsp (40 mL) of sugar.

Start Exercising

Keeping fit doesn't mean enduring long, grueling workouts. Just try to be active for an hour every day (not necessarily all at once), and do lots of different activities to benefit your entire body.

Warming Up

Launching straight into energetic activities can cause injuries, so prepare your body first. Spend five minutes doing gentle exercises to loosen and warm your muscles, get **joints** moving smoothly, and raise your heartbeat gradually so as not to strain your heart.

How many skips can you do before you're out of breath?

Warming up can involve marching, jogging, or bouncing in place...

...then lifting your arms and raising your knees higher with each step...

...and finally giving each part of your body a shake and a gentle stretch.

Healthy Heart

Any activity that makes your heart beat faster is called aerobic exercise. It strengthens your heart and helps it pump blood more efficiently throughout your body. Here's how to check your heart rate.

1. Hold out your arm, palm up. Using the first two fingers of your other hand, press down lightly just below your wrist, at the base of your thumb, until you feel your pulse.

2. Count your pulse for a minute. It should beat between 70 and 100 times.

3. Now do ten minutes of aerobic exercise and check your heart rate again. The target to aim for is about 130 beats per minute.

60 secs

Take a Deep Breath...

Regular exercise strengthens your lungs so they can hold more air and give your body extra oxygen. This helps you exercise more efficiently.

To see how much air your lungs hold, stretch a balloon, take a deep breath, then—with one exhale—breathe out all the air into the balloon. Measure the balloon, and repeat after a few weeks of exercising to see if your lungs have improved!

Don't blow so hard that you make yourself feel dizzy.

Pssst... If you're exercising with friends, warm up by kicking or throwing a ball to each other.

Super Sports

What kind of exercise do you like? Perhaps you enjoy team games with friends, or maybe you prefer solo sports. If you're really not into sports, don't despair! Try some of these ideas—one might be perfect for you.

Pssst... Get a friend to start a new sport with—you'll feel less nervous.

Clubs and Classes

Joining a sports club or class is a great way to try new things. How about a combat sport such as tae kwon do, or indoor climbing on artificial rock walls, or skiing on dry ski slopes? Fitness classes such as zumba are great if you like to dance.

Get Out and About. . .

Family hiking or camping trips feel more like vacations than sports, but they can be very energetic. Other fun outdoor sports include orienteering and geocaching, where you use a **GPS receiver** or cell phone to locate hidden prizes.

In orienteering, every time you find a marker you punch your card with the special hole punch provided.

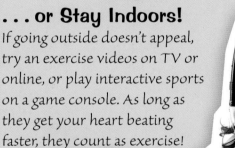

If you find a geocache, take one of the small gifts and put a new one inside. There is also a log book to fill in.

. . . or Stay Indoors!

If going outside doesn't appeal, try an exercise videos on TV or online, or play interactive sports on a game console. As long as they get your heart beating faster, they count as exercise!

Water Workout

Swimming is a great body workout, whether you go to classes, compete in races, or just splash in the pool on vacation! It can also lead to other aquatic sports, such as water aerobics, water polo, snorkeling, canoeing, or even synchronized swimming.

Strange Sports

Zorbing is a sport where people roll along the ground in a transparent plastic ball.

Canine freestyle dancing is just what it sounds like—dogs and their owners dancing together.

Other unusual sports include stair racing, swamp soccer, toe wrestling, and joggling (a combination of juggling and jogging).

Fun and Games

Exercise doesn't have to mean playing organized sports—you can make up your own games to play with your friends! Here are some super ideas for the park or backyard.

Chasing Games

Playing tag is a great way to get moving, but why not invent new rules? Perhaps people who are tagged have to lie down until someone tickles them. Or maybe everyone has to play while balancing beanbags on their heads, or carrying plastic cups of water that they can't spill!

Crazy Courses

Get creative with a backyard obstacle course! It could include doing five twirls of a hula hoop, keeping a balloon off the ground for a minute without using your hands, crawling under lawn chairs, splashing through a kiddie pool, or hanging five shirts on a clothesline as fast as you can!

Brave the Weather

Wet and windy weather doesn't have to stop you from going outside. Catch leaves in the wind, jump over puddles, or run as fast as you can from one shelter to another.

Super Snow

There's so much to do in the snow! Building snowmen, having snowball fights, or pulling a sled up a hill will get your heart racing in no time. You could also try digging a winding maze in deep snow or designing an intricate pattern with your footprints.

Pssst... Don't spoil the fun by getting too competitive. It really doesn't matter who wins these made-up games!

No-fuss Fitness

There are many ways to find time for exercise in everyday life. Get into the habit of doing some of these activities and you'll be more fit without realizing it.

Don't forget that a trip to the mall can count as exercise as long as you do plenty of brisk walking!

Help at Home

Household chores could earn you some extra pocket money as well as improve fitness. Walking the dog, washing the car, vacuuming the carpet, and raking leaves all burn lots of energy.

Walk and Talk

Try using your legs instead of your phone—could you walk to a friend's house to chat instead of texting from home? At the park, stroll as you talk rather than sit on a bench. If you're busy yakking, you'll walk miles without even realizing it!

Pssst... Get a **pedometer** to see how far you walk in a day. Think of ways to increase your daily total.

24

Amazing Music

Dancing to your favorite music is a wonderful way to exercise—and it can cheer you up, too! Listen to lively music on headphones when out walking. The beat will help you keep a brisk pace.

TV Workouts

Sitting slumped in front of the TV is terrible for your posture and makes you feel sluggish. Here are some tips for healthier TV-watching.

1. Sit up properly. This doesn't mean holding your back rigid—instead, pull back your head so your ears are above your shoulders. Relax your shoulders and keep your feet flat on the floor.

2. Do gentle stretches to avoid aches and stiffness. Hold out a leg and rotate your ankle, stretch both arms outwards and circle them, or touch your shoulders and gently pull your elbows back. Do each action a few times.

3. Get up regularly. Make it a rule that you walk or march in place during commercial breaks. If you're with friends, you could dance or do certain moves, such as hopping during toy commercials and doing jumping jacks during food ones!

Stay Safe

Staying fit and healthy means using your head and looking after yourself. Here are some tips to avoid injury and illness.

Get the Gear

Wear loose-fitting, comfortable cotton clothing for exercise. Take off jewelry and make sure you have tennis shoes that fit properly. Carry an extra layer to put on after exercise, as your body will go on sweating and losing heat, leaving you shivering.

Certain sports need special safety gear — such as a helmet for riding.

Cool Down

If you do lots of exercise then stop suddenly, your muscles may become stiff and sore. Do a few gentle cool down stretches to relax your muscles and gradually lower your heart rate.

Easy Does It

Too much exercise is bad for you—it can strain your heart and muscles, leave you gasping for air, and make you feel sick. Take it easy and stop before you're completely exhausted. Always drink plenty of water to replace the fluid your body has lost through exercise.

Pssst… Don't exercise if you're not feeling well. Give your body a few days to recover.

Outdoor Dangers

Think before heading out. Wear layers on cold days, and a hat and sun block in warmer weather. Be aware of traffic and other people around you. Make sure an adult knows where you are, and don't go on long walks or bike rides alone. Bringing a phone is also a good idea.

Wear a helmet when riding bike and stay alert near traffic and pedestrians.

Watch Out For...

Cramping: the painful feeling when muscles suddenly tense up. Try gently stretching and rubbing the area until it relaxes. Drinking plenty of water also helps.

Heat exhaustion: happens when your temperature rises so high that you feel sick and dizzy. Avoid it by drinking water and not exercising in extreme heat.

Indigestion: stomach pains that can be caused by exercising after eating, especially if you've had a big meal. Wait an hour or two after meals before doing vigorous exercise.

And Relax...

Knowing how to wind down and relax is as important for your body as diet and exercise. But this doesn't mean vegging out in front of the TV or computer for hours—it's about being calm, controlled, and composed.

Ditch the Stress

To really relax, you need to clear your head. Pick a time when you won't be disturbed by anyone. Go somewhere quiet and private, such as your bedroom or backyard. Find a comfy place.

Close your eyes and think of a relaxing image. Perhaps you're on a beach or floating in space. Breathe slowly and relax each part of your body.

Chill Out

If you're just too fidgety to sit quietly (or likely to fall asleep!) then there are many other ways to relax. Take a bath, dance, play a musical instrument, cuddle your pet, reorganize your closet, or look at old photo albums. Do whatever makes you feel calm and happy.

Listening to your favorite music may be a perfect way to unwind after a busy day.

Pssst… Think positive! Focus on things that make you feel good about yourself, and try not to worry too much.

Be Organized

Sticking to good routines makes you less likely to forget important things and then panic about them. Do homework or chores early in the day, so you're not working (or stressing) late at night. Wind down before bed by reading or writing in a diary instead of watching TV, texting, or staring at a computer.

1) Ask about project
2) Buy new earphones
3) Call Beth

Making a to-do list before bedtime can help you clear your mind and fall asleep more easily.

Goodnight

Go to bed at a reasonable time. You need about nine or ten hours of sleep every night. Without it, you'll be low on energy—and grumpy, too! And that may tempt you to eat sugary foods for quick energy bursts.

Glossary

allergic
Extra-sensitive to something, leading to bad reactions such as sneezing and skin rashes, or sometimes even dizziness and difficulty breathing.

carbohydrates
Natural substances your body needs for energy. There are two types: starch (in foods such as bread and pasta) and sugar.

circulation
The constant flow of blood around your body, pumped by your heart.

conditioner
A creamy liquid rubbed into wet, clean hair and rinsed off to help make it shiny and smooth.

crème fraîche
A type of thick sour cream. It won't separate into lumps when heated. Make your own with buttermilk and heavy cream.

dehydrated
Not having enough water in your body, which means that it can't work properly.

digestion
The process of breaking down food and turning it into chemicals that your body uses to grow and work properly.

GPS receiver
A device that picks up signals from satellites in space and uses them to figure out its location. GPS stands for Global Positioning System.

immune system
Parts of your body that work together to destroy germs and keep you healthy.

joint
A place where two bones meet in your body.

minerals
Nutrients in food that your body needs to stay healthy. Important minerals include calcium, iron, and zinc.

nutrients
Natural substances found in plants and animals that your body needs to work properly.

omega-3 fatty acids
A healthy type of fat that is found in oil from fish and some plants.

pedometer
A small electronic device, often worn on a belt, which counts every step a person takes by sensing the movement of their hips as they walk.

processed
Fresh food that has been cooked, canned, or preserved. Processing can make food safer by killing bacteria, but extra fat, salt, or sugar is sometimes added, for example, in boxed meals and cereal.

protein
A substance found in many foods that your body needs to grow and become strong.

tofu
A food made from soy beans and water, pressed into blocks that look like white cheese. Tofu can be used in both savory and sweet dishes.

vitamins
Natural substances in food that your body needs to work properly and grow strong.

Smart Sites

www.longlocks.com/hair-care-recipes-cookbook.htm
Lots of ideas for making your own natural shampoos and conditioners.

www.kidshealth.org/kid/recipes
All kinds of imaginative recipes for tasty meals and snacks.

www.allrecipes.co.uk/recipes/tag-5685/kids-smoothie-recipes.aspx
Fun, easy ideas for creating delicious fruit smoothies.

www.monkeysee.com/play/1494-fitness-for-kids-warm-up-routine
Short videos to help you warm up and exercise properly.

www.kidspot.com.au/kids-activities-and-games/fun-outdoor-activities-for-kids+9.htm
More than 100 suggestions for outdoor games and fun!

Index